This book belongs to:

Isabella
grase
Calabrese.

Retold by Gaby Goldsack
Illustrated by Ruth Galloway (Advocate)
Designed by Blue Sunflower Creative

Language consultant: Betty Root

ISBN 1-40545-559-4

This is a Parragon Publishing Book
This edition published in 2005

Parragon Publishing
Queen Street House
4 Queen Street
Bath BA1 1HE, UK

Snow White
and the
Seven Dwarfs

Helping your Child Read

Learning to read is an exciting challenge for most children. From a very early age, sharing storybooks with children, talking about the pictures, and guessing what might happen next are all very important parts of the reading experience.

Sharing reading

Set aside a regular quiet time to share reading with younger children, or to be on hand to encourage older children as they develop into independent readers.

First Readers are intended to encourage and support the early stages of learning to read. They present much-loved tales that children will happily listen to again and again. Familiarity helps children identify some of the words and phrases.

When you feel that your child is ready to move on a little, encourage them to join in so that you read the story aloud together. Always pause to talk about the pictures. The easy-to-read speech bubbles in **First Readers** provide an excellent 'joining-in' activity. The bright, clear illustrations and matching text will help children understand the story.

Building confidence

In time, children will want to read *to* you. When this happens, be patient and give continual praise. They may not read all the words correctly, but children's substitutions are often very good guesses.

The repetition in each book is particularly helpful for building confidence. If your child cannot read a particular word, go back to the beginning of the sentence and read it together so the meaning is not lost. Most important, do not continue if your child is tired or just needs a break.

Reading alone

The next step is to ask your child to read alone. Try to be on hand to give help and support. Remember to give lots of encouragement and praise.

Along with other simple stories, **First Readers** will ensure that children will find reading an enjoyable and rewarding experience.

Once upon a time there was a king and a queen. They had a beautiful baby girl.

The king and queen called her Snow White.

The queen died soon after Snow White was born.

The king was sad and lonely.

But, one year later, the king married again.

The new queen was very beautiful.

She liked to look at herself in a mirror.

The queen had one special mirror. It was magic. Every day she looked into the magic mirror and said,

"Mirror, mirror on the wall,
who is the fairest of them all?"

And the mirror would answer,
"You are the fairest."

One day, the queen looked into the mirror and said,

"Mirror, mirror on the wall,
who is the fairest of them all?"

And the mirror said,

"You were the fairest, shining bright.
But now the fairest is Snow White."

The queen was very angry.
She called for a servant.

"Take Snow White into
the forest and kill her,"
said the queen.

14

The servant took Snow White into the forest.

"I don't want to kill you. Run away, please," he said. And he walked away.

"Please don't leave me," said Snow White. He left her near a cottage.

Snow White walked to the cottage.

She knocked at the door. There was no answer, so she went in.

She saw seven little chairs around a little table. Then she saw seven little beds.

Snow White was very tired. She lay down on one of the beds.

Seven little dwarfs lived in the cottage.

Every day they went into the hills to dig for gold.

That night, they came back to the cottage.

They found Snow White fast asleep.

When she woke up she told them

her story.

"You can stay with us," said the dwarfs.

The next day the seven dwarfs went into the hills to dig for gold.

Snow White stayed at the cottage.

"Do not let anyone in," the dwarfs said to Snow White.

Back at the palace, the queen looked
into her magic mirror and said,

"Mirror, mirror on the wall,
who is the fairest of them all?"

Who is the
fairest?

And the mirror said,

"You were the fairest, shining bright.
But now the fairest is Snow White."

The queen was very angry. She put some poison in an apple. She dressed up as an old woman and went to the cottage.

Snow White opened the door and saw the old woman.

"Would you like an apple?" the old woman asked.

"Yes, please," said Snow White. She took one bite and fell to the ground.

When the seven dwarfs came home, they could not wake Snow White.
They were very sad.

The dwarfs put Snow White in a glass box.

A prince came riding by. He saw Snow White.

"What a beautiful girl," he said.

The prince opened the glass box.
He kissed Snow White.

The kiss woke her up. She saw the
prince and fell in love with him.

"Will you marry me?" asked the prince.

"Yes!" said Snow White.

One day the queen looked in her magic mirror and the mirror said,

"You were the fairest, shining bright. But now much fairer is Snow White."

The queen was so angry that she disappeared.

26

Snow White and the prince got married and lived happily ever after.

Read and Say

How many of these words can you say? The pictures will help you. Look back in your book and see if you can find the words in the story.

king

Snow White

queen

mirror

forest

prince

cottage

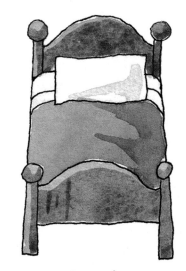

bed

dwarfs

apple